T0195841

Sammy: The Snow Eating Dog "RESCUED"

Melissa Wittasek

WestBow Press books may be ordered through booksellers or by contacting:

WestBow Press
A Division of Thomas Nelson & Zondervan
1663 Liberty Drive
Bloomington, IN 47403
www.westbowpress.com
844-714-3454

ISBN: 978-1-6642-6387-1 (sc)
ISBN: 978-1-6642-6389-5 (hc)
ISBN: 978-1-6642-6388-8 (e)

Library of Congress Control Number: 2022907233

Print information available on the last page.

WestBow Press rev. date: 04/26/2022

WESTBOW
PRESS®
A DIVISION OF THOMAS NELSON
& ZONDERVAN

Sammy: The Snow Eating Dog "RESCUED"

High up in the Colorado mountains there lived a nice family. They loved each other and loved God. The lived in a cozy cabin with a big fireplace. In this cabin were Mom, Dad, Bobby, and Susie. They loved living in the mountains.

During the summer they would fish and hike and during the chilly winter months, they would go sledding and make snowmen. The family was incredibly happy and played and prayed together.

One cold, snowy evening during dinner, dad said, "This family is so special. God has blessed us. I want to grow our family and get a dog!" The children squealed in delight! "Can we get a big furry dog?" asked Bobby. "No, I want a cute cuddly dog!" said Susie. Mom replied, "Why don't we all go to the shelter and pick one out together?"

So that is exactly what the family did. The next day, they loaded up in the car and headed to town. "Dear God," dad prayed, "please help us find the most special dog for our family."

When they got to the shelter, they were very excited to see all the dogs available for adoption. "I want this one!" cried Bobby. "He's too big." exclaimed Susie. They were very hopeful they would find the perfect dog.

Adopt a dog here

Finally, they came to the last cage. There sat a quiet, gentle dog, with sad eyes, named Sammy. Sammy was just 5 years old and had been at the shelter the longest. The family at once fell in love with Sammy. "We will take him!" exclaimed dad. Sammy had found his forever home!

See, Sammy was not an ordinary dog. In fact, the family would soon find out just how special Sammy really was...

High in the Colorado mountains, it would snow and snow. Sometimes it snowed for days. Dad kept busy shoveling and mom kept busy cleaning and cooking. The kids enjoyed playing with Sammy and watching the snow fall. Sammy loved the snow. It was his favorite thing!

What made Sammy so special was that his favorite thing, snow, was also his favorite food! Sammy loved to eat snow! Every time it snowed, Sammy would go outside and eat snow until his belly was full. Day after day, Sammy begged to go outside to eat more snow. Bobby and Susie loved watching Sammy eat snow.

One weekend after Christmas, it snowed hard for days. The snow even came down sideways. Sammy sat at the window and was very happy to see all the snow. Dad was tending to the fire and mom was cooking dinner while the kids played. And of course, Sammy was watching the snow through the window.

Dad had to go to the shed for more wood for the fire. But when dad opened the door, the snow had piled all the way to the top of the door! Dad could not get out to get more firewood. Dad tried to dig through the snow, but it just kept piling up. The family prayed together, "Dear God, please help us. We will freeze without firewood."

Just then, Sammy perked up, ran to the door and started barking. Sammy had a plan. Dad opened the door and guess what? Sammy started eating the snow! He ate and ate and ate! He chomped and filled his belly over and over.

Sammy ate a snow tunnel all the way to the shed and dad was able to get more firewood!

Finally, the cabin was warm again and the family was safe. God answered the family's prayers. Sammy had saved the day!

THE END

About the Author

Melissa started writing Christian children's books to not only entertain children, but to also express her love for God.

Printed in the United States
by Baker & Taylor Publisher Services